sound
hearing
music

"Kenmore Primary School"

sound
hearing
music

"Kenmore Primary School"

SCIENCE FACTORY

SOUND & MUSIC

JON RICHARDS

FRANKLIN WATTS
LONDON • SYDNEY

© Aladdin Books Ltd 1999

Designed and produced by
Aladdin Books Ltd
28 Percy Street
London W1P 0LD

ISBN 0 7496 3413 8

First published in Great Britain
in 1999 by
Franklin Watts Books
96 Leonard Street
London EC2A 4XD

Design

David West
Children's Book Design

Designer
Flick Killerby

Illustrators
Ian Moores & Ian Thompson

Printed in Belgium

A CIP catalogue entry for this book is
available from the British Library.

Some of the illustrations in this series
have appeared in books previously
published by Aladdin Books.

The author, Jon Richards, has written
a number of science and technology
books for children.

The consultant, Steve Parker has
worked on over 150 books for
children, mainly on a science theme.

All the photos in this book were
taken by Roger Vlitos.

ABOUT THE BOOK

Sound and Music examines the basic aspects of sound, as well as its more complex and practical uses. By following the projects carefully, the readers are able to develop their practical skills, while at the same time expanding their scientific knowledge. Other ideas then offer them the chance to explore each aspect further to build up a more comprehensive understanding of the subject.

CONTENTS

THE WORKSHOP

BEFORE YOU START any of the projects, it is important that you learn a few simple rules about the care of your Science Factory.

● Always keep your hands and the work surfaces clean. Dirt can damage results and ruin a project!

● Read the instructions carefully before you start each project.

● Make sure you have all the equipment you need for the experiment (see check-list opposite).

● If you haven't got the right piece of equipment, then improvise. For example, a washing-up liquid bottle will do just as well as a plastic drinks bottle.

● Don't be afraid to make mistakes. Just start again – patience is very important!

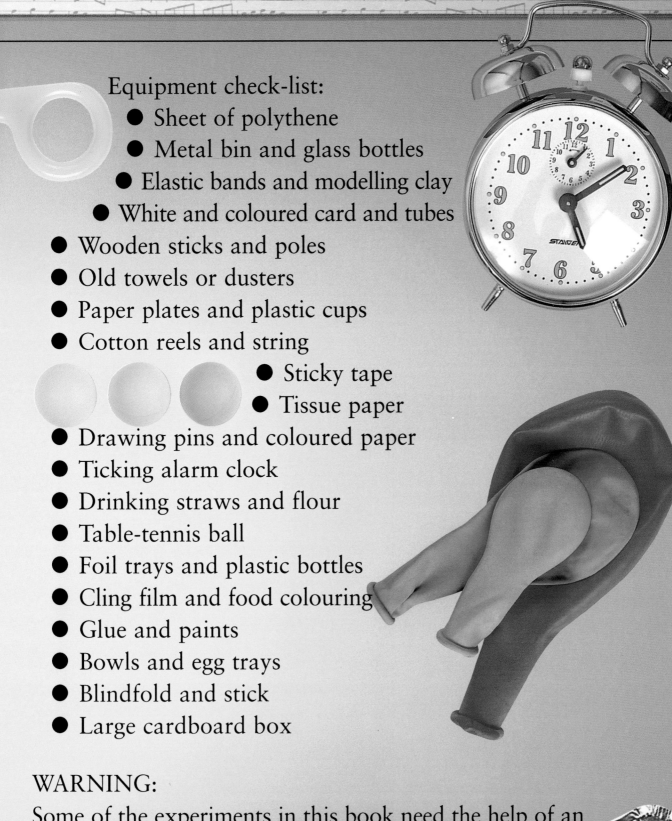

Equipment check-list:
- Sheet of polythene
- Metal bin and glass bottles
- Elastic bands and modelling clay
- White and coloured card and tubes
- Wooden sticks and poles
- Old towels or dusters
- Paper plates and plastic cups
- Cotton reels and string
- Sticky tape
- Tissue paper
- Drawing pins and coloured paper
- Ticking alarm clock
- Drinking straws and flour
- Table-tennis ball
- Foil trays and plastic bottles
- Cling film and food colouring
- Glue and paints
- Bowls and egg trays
- Blindfold and stick
- Large cardboard box

WARNING:
Some of the experiments in this book need the help of an
adult. Always ask a grown-up to give you a hand
when you are using sharp objects, such as
scissors, or electrical objects!

RIPPLES IN THE AIR

WHAT YOU NEED
Sheet of polythene
Metal bin
Elastic bands
White card
Coloured card
Wooden sticks
Paints

YOU CAN HEAR SOUNDS AROUND YOU ALL THE TIME. Whether they are the roar of a jet plane taking off or the faint rustle of leaves in a tree, sounds are always reaching your ears. But what are these sounds, how are they caused and how is it that they can travel from their source to you? This first experiment looks at how sounds are made and also explains how they travel through the air and reach your ears.

WATER WAVES

The next time you are near to a pond, carefully drop a small stone into the water. When the stone hits the water, it creates a disturbance which forms ripples on the surface. These ripples quickly spread out away from the source of the disturbance in much the same way as sound waves travel through the air.

DRUM BEATS

1 Stretch the polythene over the top of the metal bin and hold it in place with the elastic bands.

2 Wrap the metal bin with a rectangle of white card which is big enough to go right around it. Decorate this with pieces of coloured card to make a pattern.

3 Paint the ends of the wooden sticks to make your drum sticks.

WHY IT WORKS

When you beat the skin of your drum, it starts to vibrate. As the skin vibrates, it causes the air around it to shake, creating a series of shock waves of sound. These sound waves spread out from the drum like ripples on a pond. When these waves reach you, your ears change these waves into sounds which you hear.

SOUND WAVES

4 Beat the polythene skin of your drum to make a noise.

THE POWER OF SOUND

WHAT YOU NEED
Coloured card
Paper plates
Cotton reels
Wooden stick
Polythene
Sticky tape
Tissue paper

ALTHOUGH SOUND WAVES SPREAD OUT LIKE THE RIPPLES ON A POND (see pages 6-7), you cannot see them. They are invisible as they travel through the air. However, you can sometimes feel their effects, especially if they are loud enough and strong enough. Build your own sound cannon in this project and see just how powerful these sound waves can be.

SOUND CANNON

1 Make a pair of wheels for your sound cannon by sticking the paper plates onto some circles of card. Stick the cotton reels to the inside of each wheel and then push the wooden stick into the other side of the reels to make the axle.

2 Make a wide tube from a large sheet of card. Stretch the polythene over a ring of card and fix it to one end of the tube using the sticky tape. This will be the back of your cannon.

3 Cut out a circle of card big enough to cover the front of your cannon. This circle should have a small hole cut out of its middle.

4 Stick this onto the front of your cannon using the sticky tape.

5 Fix your cannon onto the wheels and weigh the back end down so that the cannon won't tip over. Now make a curtain by cutting the tissue paper into narrow strips.

6 Aim the cannon at the tissue paper curtain and tap the polythene quite hard. You should see the strips of tissue paper move as you make the noises.

8

MOVING AWAY

Move the cannon away from the curtain and find out your cannon's range when the strips stop moving.

WHY IT WORKS

When you tap the polythene it creates sound waves inside the cannon. Because of the small hole at the front of the cannon, these sound waves come out of the cannon in a narrow beam. As these sound waves hit the curtain, they cause the strips of tissue paper to move, letting you see the power of sound.

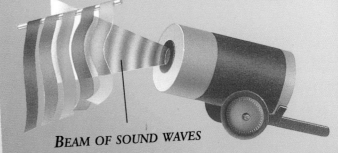

BEAM OF SOUND WAVES

KNOCKING IT OVER

Cut some skittle shapes out of paper and prop them up by folding the base of each skittle over at right angles. Now aim your sound cannon at the skittles and see if the sound waves from it are powerful enough to knock the skittles over.

BOUNCING SOUNDS

FROM THE PREVIOUS EXPERIMENTS, you have seen that sounds spread out from their source in waves (see pages 6-7) and that these waves have the power to move things and cause them to vibrate (see pages 8-9).

However, what happens to sounds when they come across a surface which is harder than a tissue paper curtain? This experiment shows you that, just like rays of light bouncing off a shiny surface or mirror, sound waves can bounce around to form echoes.

(see pages 6-7)
(see pages 8-9)

WHAT YOU NEED
Paper
Stiff card
Ticking clock

SOUND REFLECTIONS

1 Find a continuous sound source, such as a ticking clock. Prop up the piece of stiff card to make your sound wall.

2 Roll the coloured paper into two tubes. These will be your listening tubes. Place them in a 'V' shape against the sound wall.

WHY IT WORKS

The sounds made by the ticking clock are channelled down one cardboard tube. They reflect off the sound wall along the other cardboard tube where you hear this sound reflection, or echo.

10

This will only work if the sound wall is hard. If it is soft, then it will absorb the sound waves and no sound will be reflected.

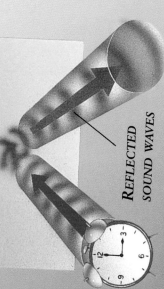

REFLECTED SOUND WAVES

CHANGING THE ANGLE

Move your listening tube around. You will find that the volume of the ticking changes. That's because the sound waves from the clock are reflected at a certain angle. Away from this angle, the listening tube picks up fewer sound waves and the volume is quieter.

3 Place the ticking clock at the open end of one of the tubes and listen at the other. You will hear that the sound of the ticking clock appears to be coming along the paper tube.

COLLECTING SOUNDS

WHAT YOU NEED
*Coloured card
Sticky tape
Pencil
String*

YOU NOW KNOW THAT SOUNDS WAVES bounce around you all the time, but do you know how they get inside your head? On either side of your head are two special sound-collecting devices – your ears! Have a close look at a friend's ears. You'll see that the outer ears are shaped like a flattened funnel – this is no accident. You can see how funnels help and improve your hearing with this experiment.

LOUD AND QUIET

Now turn the ear trumpet the other way round and you'll find that sounds become quieter. This is because very few sound waves can enter the trumpet through its smaller hole. Any that do, quickly lose their energy in the trumpet, without reaching your ear. You can also use your ear trumpet as a megaphone to make your voice louder.

4 Hold the ear trumpet to your ear and listen as it makes sounds louder.

EAR TRUMPET

1 Draw a large semicircle on the coloured card using some string and a pencil. Ask an adult to cut this semicircle out to form the template for your ear trumpet.

2 Roll the semicircle of card and stick it together so that it forms a cone which is open at both ends.

3 Fasten a strip of card to the side of the cone to act as the handle for your ear trumpet. Decorate your ear trumpet.

WHY IT WORKS

The ear trumpet collects sound waves and stops them from escaping into the surrounding air. The energy of these sound waves is then channelled into your ear. Because more sound energy reaches your ear, the sounds you hear seem louder.

13

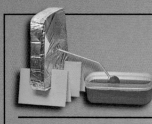

HEARING SOUNDS

THE "COLLECTING SOUNDS" EXPERIMENT ON PAGES 12-13 showed you how the funnels which form your outer ears collect sounds and channel them into your brain. But how does the ear change these sound waves into signals which your brain can understand? Build your own artificial ear and see how your complicated inner ear works.

WHAT YOU NEED
Coloured card
Bendy drinking straw
Table-tennis ball
Foil tray
Cling film
Glue
Sticky tape
Bowl of water

BUILDING AN EAR

1 Make a base for your artificial ear, big enough to support the foil tray.

2 Cut a hole from the bottom of a foil tray. Ask an adult to do this for you as the edges can be sharp.

3 Stretch the cling film over the top of the foil tray.

WHY IT WORKS

Just as the sound waves from your sound cannon made the tissue curtain vibrate (see pages 8-9), so the sound waves from your voice make the cling film vibrate. This vibrates the straw, causing ripples in the water. Inside your ear is a film called the ear drum. This vibrates when sound waves hit it, causing three tiny bones to vibrate. These create ripples in the fluid inside an organ called the cochlea. These ripples are turned into signals which are then sent to the brain.

EAR DRUM   EAR BONES   COCHLEA

4 Cut one end of a bendy straw and pull apart the halves.

5 Then cut the end of the straw nearest the bendy part and push it onto the table-tennis ball. Stick the flaps onto the ball using the glue.

6 Stick the other end of the straw to the middle of the cling film using sticky tape.

GOOD VIBRATIONS

Try testing your artificial ear with different sounds. See whether they produce different patterns of ripples on the surface of the water.

7 Place the foil tray on the stand and then place the bowl of water so that the table-tennis ball just rests on the water's surface. Now speak into the base of the foil tray and watch as the straw and ball bob up and down, making ripples in the water's surface.

STEREO SOUNDS

HAVE YOU EVER WONDERED WHY YOU HAVE TWO EARS, one on either side of your head? You've already seen how your ears collect and hear sounds, but did you know that your ears can also tell you which direction a sound is coming from? Build a paper cracker with this project and use it to test your power of sound direction detection.

WHAT YOU NEED
Large square of paper
Blindfold

PAPER CRACKER

1 Fold the square diagonally to form a triangle.

2 Fold the top right-hand corner down.

3 Fold the triangle in half. Make sure that the folded corner is on the inside.

6 Grasp the three pointed ends of the triangle together. Flick your wrist down to make the cracker work.

WHY IT WORKS

Because your ears are on the sides of your head, sounds from one side arrive at each ear at slightly different times. The sound will reach the nearest ear before the one on the far side of your head. Even though the time difference is less than one-hundredth of a second, your brain can spot the difference and work out which direction the sound came from.

4 Make a crease down the middle, but don't fold it.

5 From the open end of the triangle, fold the top layer of paper over along the crease. Flip the triangle over and repeat. Now decorate your cracker with bright colours.

7 Sit in the middle of a room and blindfold yourself. Now ask a friend to make noises with the cracker from different parts of the room. See if you can guess the direction in which your friend is standing each time.

MONO HEARING

Now try the experiment again, but this time cover one of your ears. You will find it much harder to tell which direction the sounds are coming from.

SENDING SOUNDS

WHEN A SOUND WAVE SPREADS OUT (look at pages 6-7 to see how it does this), it passes its energy on from one tiny air molecule to the next. Sound waves need these tiny molecules in order to spread out. However, sounds can use molecules from other substances apart from air. Build your own simple telephone set and see how the molecules in solid objects let sounds travel through them.

WHAT YOU NEED

Two plastic cups
String
Coloured paints
Sharp pencil

TELEPHONE LINE

1 Ask *an adult to pierce the bottoms of the two plastic cups using a sharp pencil.*

2 Decorate the cups *using some coloured paints. Add a drop of washing-up liquid to help the paint stick to the plastic cups.*

LOUD AND SOFT

Try the experiment with the string slack. You will find that no sounds travel from one cup to the other, because the string cannot vibrate unless it is pulled tight. Now try holding the cups in different places and see what this does to the sound level.

3 Thread the string through the holes in the bottom of the cups and tie each end with a knot.

4 Hold one of the cups and ask a friend to hold the other. Stand far apart so that the string is pulled tight. Now ask your friend to speak into his or her cup and you will hear what he or she is saying in your cup.

WHY IT WORKS

When your friend speaks into his or her cup, the air molecules in the cup vibrate, causing the sides of the cup and the string to vibrate. These vibrations pass along the string, eventually causing your cup to vibrate. These vibrations are detected by your ears and turned into sounds.

SOUND WAVES

VIBRATIONS

SOUND WAVES

You will find that the sounds will be loudest when the cup is held by its lip. When the cup is held by its sides, it cannot vibrate fully, so the sound is deadened.

THE SPEED OF SOUND

FROM ALL THE PREVIOUS EXPERIMENTS IN THIS BOOK, it may have seemed as if sounds reached your ears the very instant they were made. However, this is not the case. Sound waves take time to travel from one spot to the other – you might actually see something happen before you hear it! The experiments on this page let you see just how slow sound waves can be!

WHAT YOU NEED
Plastic bottle
Balloon
Elastic band
Flour
Pin

EXPLODING FLOUR

1 Ask an adult to cut the top off a plastic bottle.

2 Fix the balloon over the spout and hold it in place with an elastic band.

3 Using the bottle top as a funnel, pour some flour into the balloon.

4 Take the balloon off the funnel, inflate the balloon with air and tie the end off securely.

TIMING ECHOES

Echoes are reflections of sound off surfaces (see pages 10-11). Stand in a large building, clap your hands and see if you can time how long the echoes last as they bounce off the many walls.

Sound waves travel through the air a lot slower than light rays. In fact, light can travel nearly 300,000 km (186,335 miles) in just one second! In the same amount of time, sound can travel through the air just 333 metres (1,090 ft)! In other words, light rays travel about one million times faster than sound waves. So you will see the balloon burst before you hear it.

5 Ask a friend to stand with the balloon quite a long distance away.

6 Now get your friend to burst the balloon using the pin. You should see the cloud of flour erupt from the balloon before the bang of the bursting balloon reaches your ears.

TIMING LIGHTNING

Time the difference between when you see a lightning flash and hear thunder. Divide the time by three and you will have the distance in kilometres.

SOUNDPROOFING

WHAT YOU NEED
Egg trays
Paints
Large cardboard box
Old towels or dusters
Alarm clock

YOU HAVE ALREADY SEEN HOW SOUNDS CAN BOUNCE OFF SURFACES and how some things can amplify sounds, or make them louder. But can anything make a sound quieter, or even get rid of it all together? Blocking out sound is called soundproofing, and it can sometimes be important. Ear protectors stop loud sounds from damaging ears when people work with noisy machinery. Build your own soundproof box with this experiment and see just how sounds can be stopped.

STOPPING SOUND

1 Decorate the egg trays using the paints.

2 Line the four walls and the floor of the cardboard box with the towels or dusters.

3 Cut the egg trays to the same size as the walls and the floor of the box and place them on top of the dusters, saving one for the top.

WHY IT WORKS

The bumpy walls of the egg cartons actually break up the sound waves as they bounce around the box, making them weaker and quieter. Also, the layers of towels or dusters absorb a lot of the sound, stopping it from passing to the box walls.

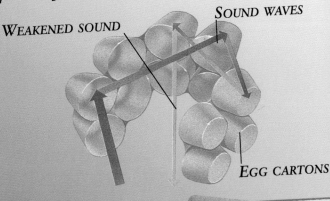

WEAKENED SOUND   SOUND WAVES

EGG CARTONS

OTHER MATERIALS

Try lining the walls of the cardboard box with other materials, such as scrunched-up newspaper or metal trays. Which work best to quieten the noise? You may even find that some of the materials will actually make the sound louder!

4 Set the alarm clock to go off in five minutes and place it inside the box. Cover it with the last egg tray and another towel or duster.

5 Close the box and listen to see if you can hear the alarm clock when it goes off. It will sound much quieter than normal, if you can hear it at all!

LOUD AND SOFT

THE LOUDNESS OF A SOUND is called its volume – the previous experiment showed you how to decrease the volume of a sound by soundproofing a box. But what actually determines the volume of a sound? Why, for example, is the roar of a jet plane much louder than the rustle of leaves in a tree? This experiment will show you how noises are made loud or soft.

PLUCK THAT BASS

1 Decorate the long wooden pole using the paints.

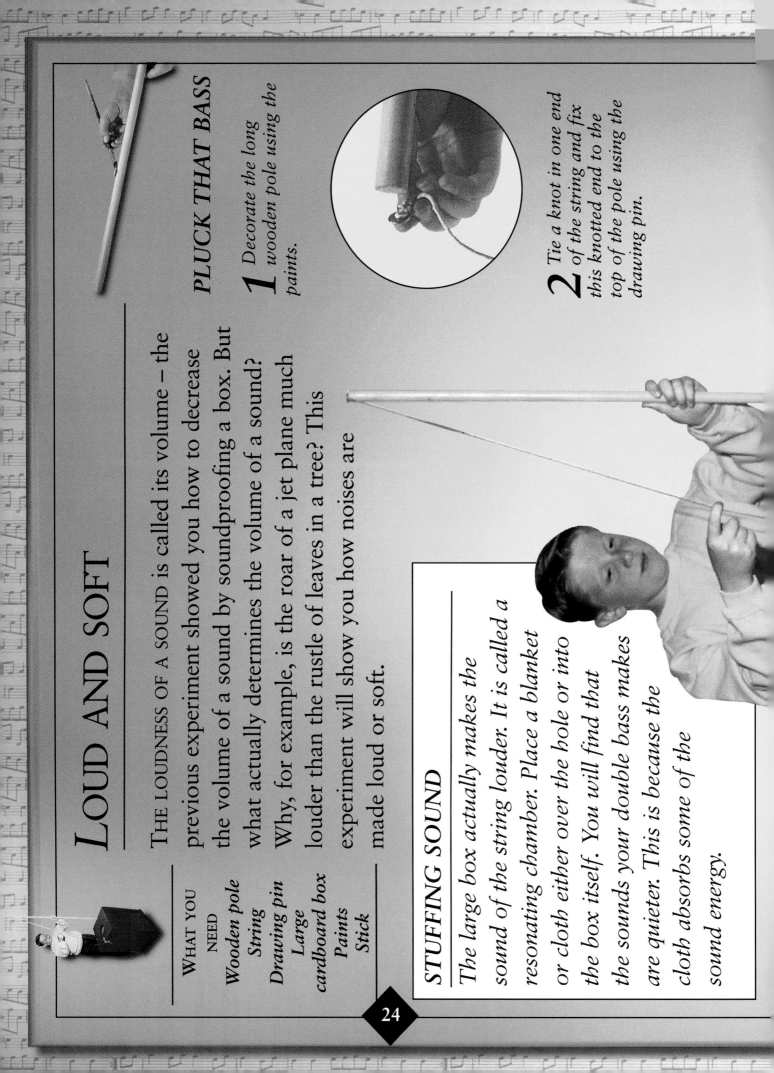

2 Tie a knot in one end of the string and fix this knotted end to the top of the pole using the drawing pin.

STUFFING SOUND

The large box actually makes the sound of the string louder. It is called a resonating chamber. Place a blanket or cloth either over the hole or into the box itself. You will find that the sounds your double bass makes are quieter. This is because the cloth absorbs some of the sound energy.

3 Paint the box and ask an adult to cut a round hole in its top. Then make another smaller hole in the top of the box and push the pole through this until it rests on the floor.

4 Ask an adult to make two small holes in the box and push the stick through, as shown here. Tie the other end of the string around the stick so that the string is tight.

5 Now pluck your string gently to make a quiet sound. Pluck it hard and the sound will be louder.

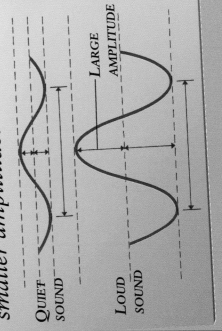

WHY IT WORKS

The volume of a sound depends on the energy put into it. The harder you pluck the string, the more you make it vibrate. This amount of vibration is called the amplitude. A loud sound will have a large amplitude, while a small sound will have a smaller amplitude.

QUIET SOUND

LARGE AMPLITUDE

LOUD SOUND

AMPLITUDE

HIGH AND LOW

NOT ONLY DO SOUNDS COME IN DIFFERENT VOLUMES, they can be high or low. How high or low a sound or musical note is is called its pitch. The pitch of a note depends upon how fast a sound wave vibrates. The speed of these vibrations is called the frequency. Faster vibrating sounds have a high pitch, while slow vibrating sounds have a low pitch. Build your own bottle xylophone with notes of different pitches.

WHAT YOU NEED
Five similar glass bottles
Jug of water
Food colouring

BOTTLE XYLOPHONE

1 *Mix some food colouring into a jug full of water. Then pour different amounts of the coloured water into the five bottles.*

2 *Place the bottles on some polystyrene or some wool. Then tap them with a spoon handle and you will find that each of the bottles has a different pitch. You can alter the water level in the bottles to change their pitch so that you can play a tune.*

WHY IT WORKS

When each bottle is hit, the column of air above the water level starts to vibrate, creating a sound.

SLOW VIBRATING SOUND WAVE GIVES A LOW NOTE

FAST VIBRATING SOUND WAVE GIVES A HIGH NOTE

The larger this column of air, the slower it vibrates, creating a lower pitched sound. So a bottle with little water in it will make a low note. A small column of air vibrates faster, creating a higher pitch.

DOUBLE BASS

Pull and push the pole as you pluck the instrument you made on pages 24-25 to make different notes.

DIFFERENT SOUNDS

FROM THE PREVIOUS PROJECTS IN THIS BOOK you have learnt the different aspects of sound, including amplitude and pitch. The last aspect is a sound's quality, or timbre. This project lets you examine the quality of a reed instrument's notes and compare it to the other instruments made in this book.

WHAT YOU NEED

Thin cardboard tube
Plastic drinking straw
Modelling clay
Paint

MUSICAL FAMILY

Using the instruments made in this book, such as the double bass from pages 24-25 and the xylophone from pages 26-27, form your own orchestra and compare the different sounds.

HOME-MADE OBOE

1 Decorate the cardboard tube using the paint.

2 When it's dry, mark holes down one side of the tube about 5 cm apart. Ask an adult to punch these holes using a sharp pencil.

3 Cut about 10 cm of the drinking straw. Squash one end of this flat and then cut a pointed 'V' shape out of this flattened end to make your 'reed'.

4 Wrap the modelling clay around the reed and insert this into the top of the tube so that it bungs the end.

28

WHY IT WORKS

The quality or timbre of a sound depends on how the note is made. When you blow into the reed, the tip vibrates very quickly. This causes the column of air in the tube to vibrate, creating a note. Other instruments make notes in different ways. A violin, for example, uses a vibrating string to make its notes.

TIP VIBRATES

REED

AIR VIBRATES

5 If your reed doesn't make a sound when you blow into it then prise the flaps apart a little. Once you can make a sound, play different notes by covering some of the holes on the sides of the tube. This changes the length of the vibrating column of air, changing the note (see pages 26-27).

FINDING OUT MORE

AMPLITUDE The loudness of a sound is known as its amplitude. *The experiment on pages 24-25 shows you how to make loud and soft sounds.*

COCHLEA The cochlea is a tiny organ found inside each of your ears. Inside is a fluid which is vibrated by sound waves. These vibrations are turned into signals which are sent to the brain where the sound is heard. *See where the cochlea is by turning to pages 14-15.*

ECHOES These are sounds which have bounced off a hard surface and can be heard after the sound has been made. *Turn to pages 10-11 to see echoes in action.*

See where the cochlea is by turning to pages 14-15.

Turn to pages 10-11 to see echoes in action.

SILENT BATS

At night, bats actually use sounds to 'see' their prey and surroundings. They squeak out sounds which are so high-pitched that we cannot hear them.

FAST AS SOUND

Chuck Yeager was the first person to fly faster than sound, at 1,078 km/h (670 mph)!

PITCH Notes can be high or low. This depends upon how quickly the sound waves which make up the sound vibrate. How high or low a note is is called the pitch. *See how you can make notes with different pitches by turning to pages 26-27.*

See how you can make notes with different pitches by turning to pages 26-27.

SOUNDPROOF A room or object which does not let sound pass through it is said to be soundproof. *The experiment on pages 22-23 shows you how to make a soundproof box.*

SOUND WAVES Sounds spread out from their source as waves, rather like ripples spreading out on a pond. *You can see how sound waves spread out by turning to pages 6-7.*

TIMBRE Notes from various instruments will have different qualities. A note from a piano, for example, will sound very different from the note from a trumpet. This quality of a note is called its timbre. *Compare the timbres of different sounds by playing the instruments which you have made throughout this book, such as the oboe on pages 28-29.*

BIG BANG

The explosion of the volcano on the island of Krakatau in 1883 created the loudest known explosion. It was heard over 5,000 km (3,125 miles) away!

NOISY WHALES

Blue whales make the loudest noises of any animal. Their underwater calls have been detected 850 km (530 miles) from their source!

INDEX